MW01277390

Blooming in the Dark

Ink Bee Publishing, LLC
P.O. Box 701
Watertown SD, 57201
InkBeePublising@gmail.com
http://authorjenleblanc.com

Cover Design by Brittany Wilson Art & Design (Brittany Wilson)
Content & Developmental Editor: (Ginger Manke)
Formatted by: Enchanted Ink Publishing (Greg Rupel)

ISBN-10: 1733000275
ISBN-13: 978-1733000277 (Paperback)

ISBN-10: 1733000267
ISBN-13: 978-1733000260 (eBook)

1st Edition 2021
10 9 8 7 6 5 4 3 2 1

Blooming in the Dark

Jennifer LeBlanc & Kirsten McNeill

INK BEE
PUBLISHING

Praise for Blooming in the Dark

"*The raw emotions encased in these pages kept me turning them for over two straight hours. These poems are full of scorching words, deep-diving emotions, and cause the reader to think deeply about who they are, their insecurities, their actions, their pasts/presents and futures. In today's day and age, words like the ones within the poems in this book are even more important as they cause you to think hard about who you are, and what you want.*"

—Josh Langlois (Author of The Supernatural Adventures of Ryan Bumble)

"*A very deep poetry collection. Serious and deep, some sad. It covers some serious issues. A few favorites of mine are Blooming in the Dark, Colours, Mosaic Me, Sunflower, and Dark Passenger. I love poetry and enjoyed this collection. I recommend it if you also love poetry, or even if you aren't into it as of yet. I think this would be a good place to start.*"

—Amanda Leigh (Author of Scarred)

"*What a great collection of poetry. So much content in this book, and so many explorations of emotion and love. The poems tend to be on the "darker" side - but emotionally, not in a gruesome manner or anything like that. A collection that, in the best traditions of poetry, dives into the surface of what it means to live. Highly recommended.*"

—William F. Aicher (Author of Scribbles and Scrabbles and Sometimes Rhymes)

"*What a pleasure to be among the audience reading the insights of each word as the writers bleed their poetry onto the page. What a captivating experience to be swept away in beautiful style masking the horrors of life. I applaud their shamelessness, a standing ovation for their courage. Read and weep. Think and become inspired.*"

-Bambi Sommers (Author of Justice Prevails)

Also by Jennifer LeBlanc

August Barton Novella Series

The Tribulations of August Barton (August Barton, #1)

The Revelations of August Barton (August Barton, #2)

Poetry

Paper Heart (Poetry Collections, #1)

Without Fear of Infamy-(Scurfpea Publishing's 2019 Annual Poetry Anthology)

Poetry is a Mountain-(AllPoetry.com's 2019 Poetry Anthology)

The Men Who Made Bonfires-(Scurfpea Publishing's 2020 Annual Poetry Anthology)

Also by Kirsten McNeill

Strength from Within

Discovering Your Worth: Happiness Through Confidence

For all those who have learned to bloom beautifully inside despite the darkness and for all those still fighting the battle.

Contents

Blooming in the Dark

Jennifer LeBlanc & Kirsten McNeill

Drowning

this sinking feeling
the overwhelming gloom
keep searching for air

Dark Reflection

like coffee stains on my teeth
you're bound to me
a tarnish never fading
and the world will never know
all the terrible things
I've done to myself for you

Unbalanced

chaos
a rising, ravenous tide
destruction
a cleansing, burning inside

when the yin and the yang
no longer represent balance
when you finally drink the potion
just like Alice

sorrow
a memory, you can't undo
darkness
a sanctuary, waiting for you

the demons within
take their turn at the wheel
while you sink deeper
at the turn of a heel

Danger Signs

what is a smile?
indicator of "*I'm fine*"
when danger is near

Fingers Crossed

I promise you
it's nothing
I promise you
I'm fine
and when
I promise you
I'm not suffering
I promise you
it's a lie

Violence Exposed

you're not the one to start the fight
but you sure as hell finish it
you swing until your last breath
and beg them to stay down
until the final blow is released
cringing as you touch the purple bruises
veins bulging from your fair skin
blood encrusted on your face and hands
barely able to move your fingers
ice is melting faster than your thoughts can cool
dripping over your aching bones
is the violence worth the agony?
the problem ever solved?
you tell yourself next time will be different
your anger will not become you
words will be your only defender
next time you will not lose control

Cruel Intent

I'm not even finished
grieving the death
of our conversation
yet you hit me
right in the self-destruct protocol
just because you could
I had almost reached
the other side of this
downward spiral
when your venom
invaded me once more
and went viral

Poison Seeps

the snake creeps up the vine
spewing lies of the divine
coiling around your pale skin
slowly crushing bones within

sharp teeth pierce the walls
releasing poison as they fall
the danger is so discreet
you continue your self-deceit

venom courses in your veins
ensuring that your strength wanes
the final strike is seen unfair
but you welcomed it without care

Siren Cry

soulful eyes
and mournful cries
don't be so fooled
by her whimpers and sighs
those aren't real tears
even though she tries
she's beckoning you
luring you in
on sympathetic nature
she relies
because she's the devil in disguise

Breaking Beauties

he compliments your beauty
as the fantasy is spun
blindly choosing to believe him
eyes sparkling like the sun

until he stops showing his affection
and it's you who is to blame
you cross lines to please him
because your delicate heart is shamed

you work to improve yourself
when he still shows no interest
his desire goes unfulfilled
you're left in the distance

Imposter Syndrome

shame on you
for teaching me
to unlove myself
so wretchedly

Elixir

I wish I could liquify
your faith in me
so I could drink it
chilled in a cocktail
and digest it
into some semblance
of self-love
I can believe

Depths Below

beneath gentle waves
black silhouettes find deeper trenches
light is out of reach

Lost in Limbo

I'm lost in all these one-sided conversations
I'm lost in my own words
lost in translation

the limbo of your inbox
is the most painful way station
I've ever been confined to

SOS I'm calling out
the beacon is lit
let me out

Deep Cuts

tears that fall
silent but there
leave words unspoken
in the air

that thing in your chest
a constant ache
longing for something
left in their wake

you can shoulder it
consume this pain
you always will
again and again

this hurt that feeds
your self-destructive needs
is an open wound
you're on your knees

but you'll be fine
you've passed the test
for now it bleeds
but it's for the best

Truth

truth falls to the floor
waiting to be recognized
bleeding from the heart

Nagging Conscience

even in the darkest places
I still find you
prodding at the wound
like a child asking too many questions

Fury's Flame

I've cried alone
lost in the dark

I know how it feels
having a gasoline heart

to burn with a need
but not know what for

to feel embers of fury
building in your core

set off by the smallest thing
only one word and the fire sings

to get so blinded by rage
hot tears spill over

to shudder and shake
and lose all composure

I've cried alone
lost in the dark

I've tried to escape
tried to find a way

to disembark
from this carousel

to leave behind
this emotional swell

this unremitting
anger and blame

but I'm still ignited
by fury's flame

Black Stain Beautiful

it does no good
to fight the hollow

so embrace your madness
take her hand and follow

where psychosis infiltrates you
where ink stains reanimate you

as black stain beautiful
inside your mind

embrace your madness
leave reality behind

False Perceptions

the past grips your neck
its contours warp your reality
these false perceptions grow
into things you can't unknow

On Your Own

the safety of their protection is gone
but was it ever really there for you?
was it even meant to last?
is there anything in it you held true?

you're on your own now
walking into every fight alone
you're on your own now
with nothing left but yesterday's ghost

the unknown begs you to proceed
unfolding an unpredictable future
the uncertainty hangs a threatening cloud
your eyes finally open

you're on your own now

Tumbling Down

from a pedestal unseen
with wavering self-esteem
tumble down
tumble down
tumble down
from glass ceilings unbroken
with failures shame awoken
tumble down
tumble down
tumble down
from mountains unscaled
with steadfast hope derailed
tumble down
tumble down
tumble down
from goals out of reach
with humility's acceptance to teach

Funeral

a smile curls your lips
thank everyone for coming
cry as you give the eulogy
laugh as others share their quips

inside you are only numb
emptiness creates its cocoon
your required emotions sit on the surface
ashamed of what you've become

she sees your struggle to feel
tells you you're not broken
grieve how you desire
there's no set path to heal

Light

deep in the ground
dirt falls on your cold body
you focus on light

Rose is a Rose

pluck the petals off the stem
you still call it a flower
crack the glass within the frame
you still call it a mirror
break the heart of a little girl
you still call her a human

The Crone

the chair creaks as she sits
wood as frail as her bones
she perches on the porch
the safest place her mind condones

fear creeps into her brain
as memories turn to dust
her previous self is dying
no longer full of life and lust

Hive Mind

they reform your choices
shaping your beliefs as theirs
chipping away at your truth
until you're part of the mold

Paper Mache Bird

she says you're disorganized
he says you're lazy
they don't know that you're tired
your memory is hazy

she doesn't see the mask
you wear because he told you to
he doesn't notice the change
when she controls what you do

you were shaped by their hand
independence chipped away with each word
picking apart then melding you back together
creating the perfect helpless bird

Living in Extremes

a ghost
or a looming shadow
too intense
or too apathetic
too on
or too off
either smothering people
or deserting them in isolation
God knows you try to hover
in that sweet spot in-between
you fail when passion is what made you
after everything that tried to break you

Disappearing Act

convinced your own beauty is subpar at best
garnering less and less of his time
no longer able to grasp his attention
all those other ones in his circle
especially the ones who can sing
put your own small voice to shame
so you stopped singing altogether
you're no match for them
fading away until you're no longer peeking
behind the curtain from backstage
silent
forgotten
invisible

Change is Cruel

when you finally learn the words to the song
they change
when you finally think you belong
the herd moves on

cruelty lies in the loss
accompanied by change
when all your straight lines
suddenly get rearranged

when you finally learn the steps to the dance
they cancel the show
when you finally think you know why
answers become things you no longer know

Lessons in Failing

first try
nothing comes of your efforts
second try
more mistakes emerge
third try
you've learned something new
fourth try
your doubts shine through

fifth try
a friend picks you up
sixth try
minor success achieved
seventh try
hesitation comes for you
eighth try
you still fail
but know what not to do

Keeping Pace

the finish line not yet in sight
putting up the endless fight

dead last, breathless, overtired
more confused of what transpired

those ahead always moving faster
you've convinced yourself of disaster

your bones aching, muscles sore
as you keep pushing from your core

and still your time is not yet here
dues unpaid always reappear

and when that finish line is gone
another in its place is drawn

Iron Maiden

I'm hardened
that's what you made me
I broke too easily
from sensitivity
now I'm the one
who does the breaking
so solid
so sharp
no one
can break through
so inevitably
I rip others open first
they can never get to me
get close enough
to cause me harm
I have no more cracks to fill
an iron maiden is what you made me

Puppet Master

the puppet master
got ahold of your strings
wanted to play
make your heart sing
wanted this dead ringer
to ring
so taught
this one heartstring was drawn
ready to snap
ready to bleed
across the sea
for them to see
boundaries unmade
vibrations incepted
as the curtain drew back
and the audience clapped
so you kept the words
his heart whispered to yours
but he took them back
and closed the doors
another piece of you gone
as you're strung along
another funeral inside
as your strings are tied

Burden Thief

sunlight is needed
> but it doesn't reach between
> it lingers there
> just outside the seams
permeated by dimness
> I lie here waiting
> pray it will find me
> the abyss is grating
my bitter heart
> growing black with time
> I embrace this pain
> but it's not mine

Come Undone

can you love me
the way I am?
can you be open
to a soul that's damned?

if I come undone
will you stay or run?
if I unveil the bullets
can you face the gun?

can you love me
the way I am?
can you let me in
can you look past my sins?

If I come undone
can you face what I've done?
If I come apart
can you know my heart?

can you love me
the way I am?
or will you turn away
from a soul so damned?

A Fools Rush

I'm a master
in the art of
premature attachment

too close
too fast
too much
to grasp

all of me
all of you
is it real?
is it true?

I give too much
you don't pull through
I have no right
you have no clue
how deep it goes
how black
how blue
I become
in the absence
of you

foolish me
it's only this
a dream disintegrating
in my fist
it burns like fire
bites like ice
ashes rain
in paradise
drifting and drifting
as reality digs
into the rift
of memory's sting

Ransom Notes

you read my scars like ransom notes
eyes full of fear and wonder
you clutch them to your chest
almost like I never left
not knowing when they'll fade
or when you'll breathe me next

Wounded

look at your wounds
sitting on display in the case
don't deny their existence
look until the day comes
when they no longer represent struggle
and you're ready to accept
the value of their presence

Radio Silent

a static goodbye repeating
this silence
is a loss
I've never known

without your voice
to carry me
to call me somewhere
that's home

Twilight Affair

my heart won't forget the space you inhabited
or the delicate sting of your eyes raking mine
or the decadent absence of illumination
that created our euphoric oblivion
through unanticipated caresses
the lustful touch of your thoughts
left handprints on my soul
a fading map of our twilight affair
and once it's gone dear Nightshade
I will always remember you there

No Vacancy

you mistook the vacancy sign above the door
for a place you could call home
but this seemingly empty room
has always been occupied
by the ghosts of others

Hope's Grave

another vulture
takes a dive

she's too used
to being used
abused
numb
immune

conditioned to know
expectations are vain
when the forecast holds promises
yet still no rain
only crushed hope
only pain

she swallows it
grain by grain
forces her lungs
to bleed and drain
as she gives up on the promises
that fill hope's grave

Vengeance Blooms

a vibrant murmur
echoes unaddressed
a soft kiss planted on your chest
right over your heart
seeds took root in the dark

a violent whisper
begs your behest
a longing seeping into your breast
sparks blooming vengeance
a sinister transcendence

a valiant request
rings true un-oppressed
a siren causing you unrest
farther and deeper this vine spreads
until you're trapped inside your head

a visceral scream
carries into your dream
a small glimpse of what could have been
drapes the memories in black
a balm for all your scars and cracks

Midnight Rage

I feel so much
I feel so hard

words split me like stones
and I break into shards

of glass reflecting
midnight rage

waiting for something
to smother my flame

Paranoid

paranoia
waking up
puts you on the fence
to keep you uneasy
you'll find no rest

paranoia
coming alive
to look for the cracks
tells you it can't be this easy
you'll find no way back

paranoia
taking over
pulls you into the unknown
give in to it deeply
you're on your way home

Evergreen

she was all crimson
brimstone and fire
burning so hot
she snapped
the high-wire

fell from grace
and drifted under
blood red empathy
where the pain
put asunder

a soul that
only knew
how to bleed
she didn't know
how to become
evergreen

Silhouette

they crave the vibrant notes of dawn
but you only sing the shadow song
they pine for a valiant perfect mask
but you're too raw for what they ask
they yearn for a fantasy come to life
but you've learned to live without the light

Dreamscape

while you sleep
it's only half a dream
of your heart's violation
a vast illusion of imprisonment
you've occupied

Transcend Oblivion

revel within me
for I am the night
tainting you
teaching you
bloom within me
for I am your light
illuminating lies
imbuing self-awareness
evolve within me
for I am your chrysalis
reforming you
re-birthing you
rise within me
for I am the night
a permanent emblem of your pain
reminding you how strong you became

Blue Party Love

I don't want you
just to want you
I shouldn't need you
I just want to
I'm a little unsure
and wholeheartedly waffling
halfheartedly taunting
can't pinpoint the itch
you always seem to scratch
I'm a junkie addicted
to the high of happenstance
and if people are drugs
I've been all smoked up
used and abused by everyone
even love
so maybe for once
just let me smoke you
until you're singing in my veins
til my lips are blue
inhale, exhale, a breath overdue
and no one can take it from me
but you

Void

fill me when I'm empty
drain me of the venom
give me all you have

Waking

a bird on the windowsill
sings a song of joy
you wish held fast in your heart

it lifts your head from the pillow
and you gather strength to stand
an action simple for most

you open the window, welcoming the song
as cool air wakes your skin
don't shrink away

the bird perches on your finger
each note connecting
keeping you from falling apart

Beware the Lunar

a creature of the night
your monster bleeds into morning
a metamorphosis you can't deny

Through the Iris

we dream in visceral color
on the most radiant frequencies
known to the subconscious entities
that haunt the ether
of our passionate manifold minds
high definition radicals
coalescing when eyelids close
and twin voids dilate
within stained glass iris encasings
to start chasing the embrace
of the oblivion of ages
each layer unfolding these internal manifestos
unlocking the prismal cages
constructed of membrane soft tissues
encompassing our immeasurable fantasies

The Ivory Dance

am I moved by the moonlight?
or is the moonlight me?
hips refracting soft ivory glow
caressing the pavement
in tandem with the dark
eyes betraying
my perception of the motion
of its silent luring
my perspective skewed
between the moon
and the illumination of this skin
I'm dancing in

Dear Darkside

when we meet again in purgatory
I hope you remember me
our sins waiting on the scale
hearts irreparably damaged
scars to remind us the pain was real
the love that carved them
worth the fate we've sealed
the agony of this flame
still ours to wield

Goodbye to You

goodbye for good this time
I won't carry you through this
goodbye to you now
I died for the last time holding on
goodbye my love
you've been too much for me
goodbye my phantom
you're finally free

Personal Penitentiary

the embrace of these chains so familiar now
they've held me for so long
my skin their memory foam
my mind the stale facility I roam
detaining me
restricted access
the binding of these shackles so comforting now
they've held me together for so long
my warden their commanding officer
my orderlies the rotting conifers
restraining me
solitary confinement
the silence of this sanctuary so loud and thunder-
ous now
bathed in sensory deprivation for so long
my heart absorbed the echoes
my soul never took them back
muting me
sensory shutdown

Relentless

forward
then back
forward
then off track
take three steps
only to fall back five
a losing fight
at first glance
but they don't know
you're not finished yet
over and over
you'll stand again
over and over
until shadows wane
over and over
to get back again
forward
then back
forward
then on track
take five steps
only to fall back three
a fortitude of will
to reach your dream

Unseen

closed doors lead to open cracks
opportunities for escape
in the most unexpected places
for those who dare to look

phantoms of doubt infiltrate you
beg you to collapse each new tunnel
attempt to drag you back down
into the silence of your comforting nook

reach past these falsities
keep seeking to find your way
there's a world out there you'll find
where you won't be overlooked

Beacon

your light weakens the feared
forcing them to cower
unable to capture or imitate your iridescence

your resilience empowers the humble

Skin Deep

they don't want you
not all of you
not who you are
not everything
just their fantasy
just a little more skin
just that smile again
that's all ladies and gentlemen
while from their eyes
it smolders and smokes
raking over you
like steaming cauldrons
left to burn at the top of the hour
because when you're pretty
you've got that power
it's all they can see
it's a blind man's disease

Pink Elephants

another sip of bubbly dreams
pass the bottle please
the pink elephants lurk
culminating static
amidst this turmoil's keep
lingering within roiling stomachs
filling up the room
when no one speaks
another sip of bubbly dreams
pass the bottle please
the pink elephants have arrived
cultivating anxiety
amidst unseen turbulence
waiting in the wings of our periphery
filling up the room
still no one speaks

Prairie Roses

planted in discord by withered hearts
a garden left unattended in the dark

thorny blossoms rooted side by side
seeds planted in vain next to rosemary and thyme

crept up through the dirt with sinister intentions
flowering in the night, a violent transgression

delicate pink petals peeled open at twilight
to reveal their bitter appetites

Hollowed

they used you up
then decided to leave
they weren't meant for you
but it's okay to grieve
you gave a lot
yet took so little
all you had
until your insides dwindled
they used you up
then left you to rust
their love was a lie
but you'll readjust
you gave a lot
yet took so little
you gave everything
yet fumbled the rush
all of you
just wasn't enough

I'm With You

your pain is not my pain
nor your story mine
but know that I am listening
you're not alone in the fight

your pain is not my pain
nor your story mine
but I still see you sinking
I know you drown at night

your pain is not my pain
nor your story mine
but I will be here anyway
until your stars align

your pain is not my pain
nor your story mine
but I believe in you
and you will heal in time

Stitched Together

I'm your new friend
we're now stitched together
from head to toe
bleeding is ignored

each moment that passes
we learn new things
risking trust
new memories scored

new stages of life
rip the threads
our fingers detach
no longer in sync

years of no contact
cause memories to fade
we're neither friends nor enemies
just strangers as we blink

Social Assault

the expectations are unfair
your heart tears

each comment is a knife
your heart cries

the smiles are all fake
your heart breaks

all your fears saturate
your heart disintegrates

Counting Sheep

words are theirs to mold
thoughts meld with the new regime
humanity feigned

Precarious You

never too far
from my mind
never too far
for me to find
you fade in
a seductive vision
you fade out
a loss a remission

never too far
from agony's embrace
never too far
for me to place
you fade in
a mask of indecision
you fade out
a wisp of superstition

How I Love You

I love you inside every shadow cast by the heart
I love you with all my darkest parts
in every secret
every scandalous thought
I love you there, where it can't be sought

it's in my bones, a residue
when I dream, I'm lost in you

I love you with each breath hitched in fear
I love you alone when no one is near
in every crevice
cracked and stained
I love you there, where our beasts were slain

It's in my marrow slithering
when I'm lost and withering

I love you inside all these burned up pages
I love you from all my darkest places
within every deception
through ash and dust
I love you there, where our souls first touched

Chasm

I blame myself
for the widening
of this chasm
It was just a slip
a short-lived spasm
of a vivid daydream
where our souls
were perceived
as effortlessly
stitched together
but even this
couldn't last forever
it was just
a temporary tether
to someone who sees
everything in me
and if I must
I'll bite back my lust
let the words
fade and rust
as reality carves rivets
into my chest
one more scar
to join the rest

Regretting Me

if you give me your love
I won't tell it to stay

one taste of my scars
it'll be on its way

one breath of my chaos
it'll come back flayed

if you give me your love
you'll regret me someday

Catch & Release

forego the ones who made you feel minor
reaping the benefits of your love
exercising their right to manipulate
expressing feigned appreciation
dominating the conversation
open your eyes to the reality
maybe this one's not who you need

Draw the Line

the line in the sand
between virtue and madness
an aging tale
teeming with controversy
discover someone's secrets
and you're marked a traitor
no room to make a single mistake
banned for life from one misstep
when errors create our decisions
boundaries are crossed
chaos erupts like wildfire
rules no longer matter
because we decided it to be
we draw the line at perfection
nothing more or less can be seen

Leave

listen to your aching heart
evade the shackles you don't deserve
abolish self-deprecation
villains of your past reaching farther
escape the fate that isn't yours

Loving Devils

my resolve
my faith
my belief in you
used to be fool proof
until I encountered
your darkness

your devilish grin
your eyes full of sin
a song you sung
with your forked tongue

to lure me
to lull me
to push me
to pull me
into your arms
where you inflicted
a most devilish harm

Matter

M.aybe
A.ll you wanted
T.hat no one could see
T.hat got overlooked
E.veryday
R.eally was to matter

Starfall

eternally plummeting
getting lost inside your eyes
pools of desperation
siphoning my shine
corroding my stars to bedrock
just so you can stay alive

Love Me

new love heart flutters
emotions are not returned
lonely without him

Fire & Ice

fire
surges within
raging of war
our crimes connect us
create the source of vehemence
break the chains
commit to happiness
our love
ice

Detox

I thought I only needed
a little space to grow
a little distance from you
to re-evaluate my road
to rethink my path
to do some soul searching
but it wasn't just a temporary
hiatus from you
I was yearning for
it was a permanent cleansing
of your toxicity
that bled into
every open pore I had
filling me with your black
filling me with your wicked
weighing me down
leaving me sickened
I know it's all just
a matter of perception
but I had to force you out
for my own protection
scrub you out
to rid myself of the doubt
caused by your judgmental asphyxiation

I refuse to be brought to my knees
by association
because I know I'm worth more
because I don't believe you anymore
and now that you're gone I can breathe again
I knew all along you were never my friend

The Offering

offer a sacrifice
to ease anxiety
until you feel brave

New Love

he is what you wanted
the purest form of love
yet you question his motives
because of former flames

your ember has never burned brighter
with the new candle on your windowsill
but insecurity catches you
secretly speaking past lovers' names

you tell yourself his words are true
his embrace is tighter more secure
comforting through the winter storms
he won't play those foolish games

Stage Left

she'll exit stage left
before you can blink
she's more perceptive
than you think
she'll fall too hard
if you draw her in
she'll love you to ruins
before it begins
she'll love you to death
with no regrets
she's a desolate universe
a goddess bereft
always searching for the one
who exited stage left

The Purge

you already started leaving in my mind
in all my anger, resentment and pride

that burned you up, turned you to ash
purged you from my thoughts
a dissolving trance

I already started fading from your heart
in all your agony, longing, and strife

that burned me up, turned me to ash
purged me from your dreams
an empty glass

Moonflower

deprive me of the light
and I'll learn to adapt
I will grow despite the darkness
I will bloom in defiant glory

Battle-worn

open your creases
gently nudge your cracks together
uncover your edges
reveal your gouges and craters
see who you are
beautifully battle-worn

Harpy Ascending

unfortunate hearts
plummet from grace
irreparable parts
ignorance can't face

but I'm still an angel
embraced by my burning
bent halo, wings mangled
from ashes returning

unfavorable odds
hold the sands of time
but not even the gods
can claim what's mine

Sensitivity

giving in to your sensitivity
makes you empathetic to animosity
seeing lives roll on in negativity
yet the simple pleasures are tranquility

the smiles and laughter are a gift
to every soul that you lift
swaying like a boat adrift
ignoring the potential rift

look into the brightest eyes
and see the darkness in disguise
trapped in a cage of its own demise
vanquished by the holder of its lies

the ones left with nothing
have the most hope to bring
learn from every song they sing
offer remnants of light to everything

Spiral Down

you keep picking at the scars
never letting the scabs heal
to remind yourself of the darkness
and what it was like to feel

it doesn't have to be this way
your healing could start now
time kissing away the pain
instead of letting you spiral down

disconnect from your oblivion
shame cannot force you undone
you're stronger than before
count the days until scars are none

Backpedal

face the inner demons
begging you to fall back
tugging at your weakness

holding the hand of a friend
rejuvenates your strength
shields your secrets

clutch your power tightly
never lose what you had
accept your uniqueness

Unclaimed Angel

you see an angel
the halo glows
your souls entwine
the connection flows

the halo breaks
you're left with emptiness
memories warped
of the emotional bliss

waking the tempest
your angel is reborn
the tainted one
you were destined for
you want her
but you shut the door

Hours of the Night

spend your life as a night owl
locked away from your enemies
reclusivity becomes your only friend
whittling away the hours of the night

loneliness whirls through your lungs
every breath a cry for help
you dug this grave for yourself
withering within the hours of the night

a beacon calls out to you
one you thought you didn't need
hold tight to the safety line
as you escape the hours of the night

Darkness

when the demons spoil your mind
foster hope that tomorrow shines brighter
rebel against uncertainty that drains your energy
kick down the notion that this is impossible
neglect the doubting voices clouding your thoughts
express your gratitude to the smallest successes
see your worth in every light that reaches you
sing with an open heart and rise within the darkness

Surging Tides

the energy within you overflows
bursting from every crevice
can't contain the electrified light
surging from your bones

the moment passes suddenly
cutting you off at the knees
you're sinking into the ground
slogging through anxiety

you're a puddle slowly freezing
clouded by the impurities
struggling to grasp shattered thoughts
lost in what you've been believing

the energy within you dies
nothing left of the luminescence
yet you choose to pick yourself up
and silence the echoing cries

Intensity

you feel too much
or
you feel too little
crying to fill the cracks
but never reach the middle

all the way up to eleven
or
bottoming out at zero
crying to fill the cracks
but never anyone's hero

Shoveling Shadows

you dig the shovel into your soul
heaving the grains out
piece by piece

until there's nothing left
and still you dig
when you cannot find release

Signs of Life

only in true darkness
do we see the light
a bright star shining
just out of reach
a spark of hope
yet the heart keeps searching
for signs of life
in the blackest nights

Lifeline

birth fosters innocence
then youth taints her mind
teens teach her to rebel
searching for something she can't find

her twenties grant her clarity
making money and having fun
creating a career to be proud of
but her work is never done

a new family is established
husband and baby take all her time
regrets of youth come and pass
never truly leaving her mind

old age is imminent
making her believe it's over
her worth is from accomplishments
judged only by those around her

she recalls the steps that brought her here
every decision was hers to make
she's a combination of darkness and light
harboring wisdom others may forsake

Your Lane

control your own actions
worry not of her missteps
or his treachery

Human Nature

hearts combine with interests shared
tainted by feathers of the Devil's wings
masking symptoms of the serpent's venom
activating instincts to protect the truth
nurturing the qualities we loathe
varying ideals threaten precious harmony
testing the limits of our compassion
yesterday becomes today's casualty

Selfish

take what you need
don't leave anything for them
see who stays with you

What If?

what if I can't take it to the next level
build something worthy of my name
conquer the darkness shadowing my frame

but what if I can earn my stature
build an empire from the ground up
claim fame and reach the golden cup

what if?
what if?
what if?

Reformation

I breathe empathy

inhale
rejection
hostility
anguish

exhale
acceptance
forgiveness
love

I take it all in
choke down the dark
digest it
transfigure it
create sparks
the light is blinding
that I bleed
through this copulation
of humility and greed

Taking Back Wonderland

I'll harness the night
learn to make it my own
unfaltering
unfailingly
with sure intentions
leaving me forever changed
to the point of misinterpretation
unrecognizably resilient
I'll wield it with certainty
irrevocably
irreversibly
striking with precision
I'll own this plight
rise within its depths
to the point of courageous intimacy
tendrils of darkness weaving
through veins on fire
unbelievably
unwinding
chains that bound me there like anchors
in despondency all along
I'll re-frame this uncertainty
reclaiming my wonderland
with phantoms commanded by my hands

Steadfast

hold on to your dignity
diminish the whispers of false intentions
level the playing field with resilience
perpetuate strength through vulnerability

Healing

your soul is torn
the best parts of you depleted
moving forward feels impossible
your will has been defeated

time renders a gentle needle
threading you back together
proclaiming your life matters
pulling at the holes until you're unsevered

for the first time since it happened
you let the sunlight grace your skin
embracing your disconnected parts
so the healing can begin

Surrender

give yourself to the emotions
rage erupting through the pores
intoxicating the broken veins
enveloping the raw sensations
find the calming relief

Mirrored Souls

eyes in transition
from hue to hue
I see the storm
inside of you
the same one
writhing
inside of me
mirrored souls
only we can perceive
the harrowing division
of love from belief

Deceptive Lover

present her the roses
the chocolates
the jewelry
share your heart

watch her pluck petals
devour the treats
put on airs
pick your love apart

open your eyes to the truth
the deceit
the manipulation
the trivial words

you come back again
for more lust
more desire
and a love that wears
the face of a liar

Words You Say

I won't cast you aside
you say
as you're walking backwards
I'll embrace you on your darkest day
you say
as your grip loosens around me
let me take your pain away
you say
as the thunderheads build above
I'll take you as you are today
you say
as you chisel at my bones

Remorse Junkie

pack up your apologies
save them for your next betrayal
to swear you should be forgiven

don't leave them at my feet
save them for whoever's next
fleeting remorse for hands you've bitten

pack up your apologies
save them for the mirror
to finally see who's the villain

Savage

S.tings doesn't it?
A.lways hurts worse coming
V.iciously from behind
A.t the very moment my
G.enerosity is taken for granted
E.clipsing all the good faith I had in you

The Wishing Well

I used to reside in
got stale after months
of choking on your duplicity
but I wasn't about to
throw my hands up in defeat and vomit
I consumed it with gusto
like gasoline
and started to climb

Hyacinth Rising

the seed was not planted in her at birth
the seed was planted from the first hurt

the seed took root at the first betrayal
the roots held tighter as she grew unstable

lies and deceit
wash rinse repeat

anger and pain
fist to face is lain

each word a lashing to the heart
chipping away all her lovely parts

bittering all her sweet
you wash rinse repeat

in a game she can't beat
there's a darkness reborn

of vengeance and rage
a new flower is thorned

when it's all over
she won't wither in defeat

and when it's all over
no more wash rinse repeat

you planted and tended
made broken and mended

the most volatile flower ever to bloom
and now your creation will be your doom

Embracing Demons

wrap your arms around the devil
tell him to find another way
a new solution to convey
shred the contract between you
welcome the brand-new day

Wounds Revisited

the memory strikes
lightning in your veins
an electric pain

choices that defined you then
the second strike
it's back again

the wounds revisited
the storm clouds clear
rise stronger
strike harder
evaporate your fear

Mending

although the battle scars remain
the agony is no more
the dragon is slain

although you look back in disdain
the ache is no more
the longing is in vain

although you ponder love's domain
the sorrow is no more
the desire is refrained

although you see this heart unchained
the enrapture is no more
the script has changed

Dark Passenger

there are days
when your dark passenger
creeps in at the edge
ink spilling onto the canvas
until everything is red
progress comes undone
hope becomes dead
as you crave the blade
the bite
the sting
the violation of flesh
but you look at me
and I am home
and the passenger knows
you're not alone
I'll ignite in you
breaking up the dark
I'll show you the truth
hiding in your heart

New Flame

the final light dims
silence envelopes the room
the new flame ignites

Driving Forward

turn on the ignition
roll down the window
check your mirrors
let the wind flow

speed down the road
without looking back
forget your history
remember what you've packed

a new chapter awaits
no new passengers at the gate
slam your foot on the pedal
driving forward to what awaits

don't pick up new commuters
or make unplanned stops
slam your foot on the pedal
driving forward to the top

Remember This

remember when it was easier
when the blame could fall elsewhere
the choices were black and white
every decision presented as fair

you chose what blade relieved your pain
extracted the self-pity and the raging fire
but that solution was a bandage
where no healing could transpire

the hardest decision was to heal
admit that you held all the cards
to unfurl the hatred inside you
and forgive yourself for the scars

Forgiveness

forgiveness
a path
not easily followed
until pressure is erupting
built up through your being
stuck in every crevice
ready to detonate
gaining traction
releasing

Uncaged

they strike you down
with idle hands
you clench your fists
ruin their plans

they taunt and tease
with insidious needs
you clench your teeth
rise from your knees

they trap you here
with quid pro quo
you look away
just let go

they taunt and tease
with jealousy's decree
you walk away
finally freed

Repeat After Me

love yourself as you would your lover
invite appreciation into your mind
give yourself credit for starting to heal
happiness is the face of new beginnings
tell yourself this truth until you believe it

Love's Eye

love is clarity
a truth
without dividends

love can see
everything
that is pretend

it knows when you
lie
cheat
steal

it knows
the overwhelming
regret you feel

love is a light
a guide
without end

love can see
everything
that is pretend

it knows when you
falter
break
conceal

It knows
the undeniable
pain you feel

Self-Love

self-love
never dies
when it comes
from a sure place
streaking across your battered plains
searching for a tranquil home
trustworthy acceptance
open your arms
reborn

Glass Half Full

see the diamond paradise
listen to the crashing waves of freedom
inhale the saccharine flowers of peace
taste the marinade of sweet memories
embrace the key to new hope

Reunion

reunion in ten years
prove yourself worthy
run through the rankings
embellish the truth

reunion in twenty years
versions of the last decade forgotten
your lies have unraveled
the pressure increased

reunion in thirty years
you're finished with games
your attendance doesn't matter
happiness is in the now

Building Blocks

the first brick is the heaviest
you don't know where to start
it cracks from minor impact
crumbling apart

you reach for a stronger one
it doesn't look quite right
paint it with shapes and colours
fill it with your light

when it's time to choose the next
find one with some zeal
your identity must be solid
when it's time for the reveal

Colours

colours
bleeding together
dripping from paintbrushes
symbolizing your ever-changing emotions
splashing new ideas of empowerment
merging with your self-worth
illuminating your vibrance
captivating stories
living

Mosaic Me

bone shards of every color
each one a different shade
I study them every night
know something more can be made
I'll break and bend
re-attach and mend
each and every piece
as a reminder
as a release
however long it takes
to sort through crystal mistakes
each color
a different season
each one
a deafening reason
to create a new mosaic
one I can believe in
so picturesque
they coalesce
into a woman I have never seen
into this new stained-glass art
that is me

Leap of Faith

sharp rocks lay below
jumping is your last escape
hope lingers nearby

A New Path

take a step towards the unknown
a path you've yet to follow
let the shadows take solid form
listen to the echoes of your misgivings

wrap the mistakes around you
embrace every moment of weakness
cut ties with the hate-filled enemies
and open your expanding wings

soar through the clouds of self-acceptance
construct your mindset of lasting light
let go of those who cannot move forward
misguided faces lost in the night

Lucky Penny

toss the penny in the wishing well
shut your eyes and dream
believe your magic casts a spell

take your hope everywhere you go
spread it to those in need
allow karma to flow

your lucky penny is your mind
send positive thoughts to others
trust you won't be left behind

Transformation

dark
ever present
feasting on insecurity
searching for your sanctity
know who will guide you
save you from yourself
highlight your worth
see your
light

Sunflower

if you ever lose the sun
face me
I'll share my light with you
if you ever forget why you came
take my hand
I'll remind you
if you ever feel doubt creeping in
pull me close
I'll fight it with you
if you ever wonder if you're enough
listen to me
"You are."

The Night Remembers

through every round in our game
of lip lashing and bloodletting
through every reverb of emotions
spun into forgiving and forgetting

it's every absence of light
like smoke hovering
in every dark corner at night
that remembers

A Letter to the Dark

shrouded in you
fear once filled me

drowning in you
my thoughts deceived me

encompassed by you
agony received me

embraced by you
finding hope wasn't easy

enlightened through you
I hope you never leave me

One

all it takes is one

one person to see you

one soul that speaks to yours

one mind that understands

one conversation

on a deserted street corner

with someone you don't know

yet felt you've known for lifetimes

one missing piece

to make the puzzle that is you

whole again

Balance

darkness and daylight
trading voices of reason
creates consonance

Resurfacing

with a shuddering breath
exhale the grip of death

with a cowering heart
embrace a new start

with a weary soul
regain control

with a faltering grasp
your defeat has lapsed

with healing wounds
resurface from this tomb

Brave

B.ravery is not the lack of fear
R.ender your failure into fuel
O.verturn uncertainty holding you back
K.eep gluing your parts together
E.nd your suffering with hope
N.ever mistake bravery for reckless action

Among The Living

BREATHE
to remind yourself
you're still alive

PRAY
to protect yourself
from uncertainty

FEEL
to encourage yourself
and let your heart be full

The Flower

flower
blooming vibrancy
flourishing with serenity
captivating every distant eye
rising towards the endless sky
the delicate petals shrivel
recede to dust
rise again
beautiful

Blooming in the Dark

she's a curious culmination
of wits, venom, shadows
she's so wild
perceives it all so deep
her roots are all tangled
and her heart you can't keep
she's too primal
too unruly to stay mild
if you intercept her in the dark
give her your love
but don't fan the spark
you'll lay abandoned
when morning comes
she'll leave your lust in the oil drum
a phantom lover you won't soon forget
can't play for keeps with sweet regret
she's so beautiful, wistful, unbending
a constellation of wounds still mending
she blooms only in dark places
and takes the shape of many faces
she's a moon flower thriving in the night
and out of the darkness
blooms beautifully bright

Authors Note

We want to thank you for reading our collection of poetry *Blooming in the Dark*. We had a lot of fun writing it together. It was definitely a labor of love and we are so proud of this project. As with many self-published/indie authors, we rely on our readers to help spread the word.

We hope you enjoyed all of the poems, but understand if some spoke to you more than others. Regardless of whether you enjoyed them all or just one or two, we appreciate you taking the time to read it. If you would be so kind as to leave an honest review at the online or instore retailer you purchased it from, it would mean the world to us.

Thank you all!

XOXO-Jen & Kirsten

CONNECT WITH JENNIFER

Author Email: jleblancbooks@gmail.com

Website: http://authorjenleblanc.com

Request Signed eBooks: https://www.authorgraph.com/
authors/jleblancbooks

Goodreads: https://www.goodreads.com/author/
show/16060895.Jennifer_LeBlanc

YouTube: https://www.youtube.com/channel/
UCiBwMZy6f_S1PkkOs8zGnKA

LinkedIn: https://www.linkedin.com/in/
jennifer-leblanc-70980a16a/

Shop Books & Merch: http://authorjenleblanc.com/shop

Twitter: @jleblancbooks

Instagram: @jleblancbooks

Pinterest: https://www.pinterest.com/inkbeepublishing

Tumblr: https://authorjleblanc.tumblr.com

Facebook: https://www.facebook.com/jleblancbooks

AllAuthor: https://allauthor.com/profile/jleblancbooks

Bookbub: https://www.bookbub.com/authors/
jennifer-leblanc

About the Author

Jennifer LeBlanc is a Multi-Award Winning, Best-selling Indie Author and Poet. Born and raised in South Dakota, she has always had a wild imagination and a knack for story-telling. When not slaying zombies in the gaming world or writing, she can be found getting lost in a good book, doing something crafty, indulging in photography, or watching movies with her husband, two cats, and long-haired chihuahuas. Jennifer loves animals, poetry, music, art, and all things creative. She currently works in merchant banking and credit services while writing her next project. In addition to working full-time and being a writer Jennifer is an Ambassador for TaleFlick as well as an Affiliate for Geekify Inc.

CONNECT WITH KIRSTEN:

Author Email: km@kirstenmcneill.com

Website: https://kirstenmcneill.com/

Goodreads: https://www.goodreads.com/kirsten_p_mcneill

Twitter: https://twitter.com/writer_kirsten/

Instagram: https://www.instagram.com/writer.kirsten

LinkedIn: https://www.linkedin.com/in/kpmcneill/

Facebook: https://www.facebook.com/writer.kirsten/

About the Author

Canadian Self-Published Author **Kirsten McNeill** strives to connect with people through her words and inspire the world to reach its full potential. Her stories and poetry are based on her own knowledge and experiences. Though they are mostly fictional, they speak her truth about today's societal pressures and the world we live in. In her spare time, she runs her own blog, plays piano and guitar, and hangs out with her family. She fully supports all things artistic and creative as she speaks her mind and lets her own creativity flow into words on the page.

Writing Playlist

Listen on Spotify:

https://open.spotify.com/
playlist/6tsTEks8A4hmADkMszdlR0

The Dark of You-Breaking Benjamin

Coming Undone-My Darkest Days

Mad World-Smash Into Pieces

Careless Whisper-Seether

Broken Pieces-Apocalyptica feat. Lacey Sturm

Lucid Dreams-Juice Wrld

Beautiful Oblivion-Issues

Tapping Out-Issues

Hanging On-Ellie Goulding

Waves-Mr Probz

Someone You Loved-Lewis Capaldi

Before You Go-Lewis Capaldi

Dancing on My Own-Calum Scott

Prayers-Slaves

Heavier-Slaves

I Know a Lot of Artists-Slaves

Trip the Darkness-Lacuna Coil

I'm Gonna Show You Crazy-Bebe Rexha

Dark Side of Me-Coheed and Cambria

Apocalypse-Cigarettes After Sex

Business of Paper Stars-Hawthorne Heights

The Waiting One-All That Remains

Dare You To Move-Switchfoot

Right Here-Ashes Remain

Already Over-Red

Hurricane-I Prevail

Scars-I Prevail

I'll Be Okay-Nothing More

Here's to the Heartache-Nothing More

Don't Stop-Nothing More

Stuck in Your Head-I Prevail

Darkside-Alan walker Lyric Terjemahan

You're Not Alone-Lacey Sturm

Scars-Tove Lo

Made in the USA
Monee, IL
28 April 2022

94876174R00098